Frogs

Annalise Bekkering

W WEIGL PUBLISHERS INC.
"Creating Inspired Learning"
www.weigl.com

Published by Weigl Publishers Inc.
350 5th Avenue, 59th Floor
New York, NY 10118
Website: www.weigl.com

Copyright ©2011 WEIGL PUBLISHERS INC.
All rights reserved. No part of this publication may be reproduced, stored in a retrieval system, or transmitted in any form or by any means, electronic, mechanical, photocopying, recording, or otherwise, without the prior written permission of the publisher.

Library of Congress Cataloging-in-Publication Data

Bekkering, Annalise.
 Frogs / Annalise Bekkering.
    p. cm. -- (Watch them grow) (World of wonder)
 Includes bibliographical references and index.
 ISBN 978-1-60596-925-1 (hard cover : alk. paper) -- ISBN 978-1-60596-926-8 (soft cover : alk. paper)
-- ISBN 978-1-60596-927-5 (e-book)
1. Frogs--Juvenile literature. 2. Tadpoles--Juvenile literature. I. Title.
 QL668.E2B416 2011
 597.8'9--dc22
                          2009050954

Printed in the United States of America in North Mankato, Minnesota
1 2 3 4 5 6 7 8 9 0 14 13 12 11 10

042010
WEP264000

Editor: Heather C. Hudak
Design: Terry Paulhus

All of the Internet URLs given in the book were valid at the time of publication. However, due to the dynamic nature of the Internet, some addresses may have changed, or sites may have ceased to exist since publication. While the author and publisher regret any inconvenience this may cause readers, no responsibility for any such changes can be accepted by either the author or the publisher.

Every reasonable effort has been made to trace ownership and to obtain permission to reprint copyright material. The publishers would be pleased to have any errors or omissions brought to their attention so that they may be corrected in subsequent printings.

Weigl acknowledges Getty Images as its primary image supplier for this title.

CONTENTS

4 What is a Frog?
7 All Kinds of Eggs
8 Waterbed
10 Inside the Egg
13 Pollywogs
14 Growing Up
16 Full-grown Frogs
18 Finding Food
20 Frogs Around the World
22 Frog Life Cycle
23 Find Out More
24 Glossary/Index

What is a Frog?

Have you ever seen a small animal hop from the water onto land? This may have been a frog. Frogs are amphibians. Most amphibians are **cold-blooded** animals. They live on land and **breed** in water.

Like all animals, frogs have a life cycle. They are born, grow, and have babies of their own.

Some frogs **burrow** into the ground when the weather is cold. This helps them stay warm.

All Kinds of Eggs

Can you imagine having thousands of brothers and sisters? Some frogs lay up to 20,000 eggs at one time. Others lay only 20 or 30 eggs. The size, shape, and number of eggs is different for each kind of frog. Only a few eggs will become frogs. **Predators**, such as birds and fish, eat the others.

Frogs only mate if the air and water are a certain temperature. For this reason, eggs are laid at different times of year.

Most frogs leave their eggs after they are laid. The male Darwin's frog keeps the eggs in its mouth. The young frogs stay there until they are **froglets**.

Waterbed

Have you ever seen clumps of small, soft balls in lakes or ponds? These may have been frog eggs. Most frogs lay their eggs in water. The eggs form a clump or strand called frogspawn.

Frog eggs are covered with a clear jelly. This keeps the eggs moist and slippery. Large masses of slimy eggs are harder for predators to eat.

Marsupial frogs keep their eggs in a pouch. When the eggs hatch, the female frog opens the pouch, and the **tadpoles** fall into the water.

9

Inside the Egg

What is the tiny black speck in the center of a frog egg? It is the baby frog, or tadpole. Over time, it grows **gills**, **organs**, and a tail.

In warm places, eggs hatch two to three days after they are laid. In colder parts of the world, eggs may take up to 40 days to hatch.

Tadpoles wriggle their way out of the egg. Then, they stick to weeds or grass found in the water. After a few days, the tadpoles start to swim and eat **algae**.

Pollywogs

Do you look like your parents? Human children look like young adults. Tadpoles look very different from full-grown frogs. They look more like small fish.

Tadpoles are also called pollywogs. They live in water and wiggle their tail back and forth to move. Tadpoles need to eat often to help them grow into frogs.

After about four weeks, tadpoles begin to change. This change is called **metamorphosis**. Skin grows over their gills. The tadpoles also get small teeth, which they later lose.

Growing Up

What happens to your body as you age? You grow in size and look older. As they grow, tadpoles begin to look more like adult frogs.

At six to nine weeks, tadpoles become froglets. First, they grow hind legs. Then, the tadpole grows front legs and lungs. The tadpole's tail shrinks as well.

By about 12 weeks old, froglets can live above the water. The tail is a tiny stump that soon disappears. Froglets are full-grown frogs at 12 to 16 weeks of age.

Full-grown Frogs

How far can you jump? Some frogs can leap up to 20 times their body length. This is because they have long, strong back legs.

Frogs drink and breathe through their skin. They keep their skin moist so it can absorb water and **oxygen**.

Frogs are ready to mate in spring. Male frogs croak using **vocal sacs** under their mouth. These calls **attract** female frogs.

Finding Food

Can you pick up your food with your tongue? Many frogs catch their food with a long, sticky tongue.

Frogs eat any live food they can find. They eat insects, snails, spiders, small fish, and worms. Larger frogs even eat mice and snakes.

Many frogs do not have teeth. They swallow their food whole.

Frogs Around the World

What if you could live on land and in water? You could live almost any place on Earth. Frogs live on every continent in the world, except Antarctica. They can live any place there is fresh water.

Some frogs spend most of their life in the water. They have feet to help them swim. Other frogs live in the desert. These frogs have thick skin. They live in burrows and only come out when there is rain. Many frogs live mainly on land. They return to the water only to mate and lay eggs.

Frog Life Cycle

Supplies

green, blue, and brown paper

white paper

black marker

tape

scissors

1. Draw a tadpole on the brown piece of paper. Cut it out.
2. Draw a froglet and an adult frog on the green paper. Cut out both of them.
3. Draw circles on the white paper, and cut them out. These will be eggs. Use the marker to make a black dot in the center of each egg.
4. Draw a half circle on the blue paper and a half circle on the brown paper. Cut both out, and tape them together to form a whole circle. The blue is water, and the brown is land.
5. Place the eggs, tadpole, froglet, and adult frog around the circle in the order they grow and the place where they live.
6. Draw arrows around the circle to show the order of the frog's life cycle.

Find Out More

To learn more about frogs, visit these websites.

How Stuff Works
http://animals.howstuffworks.com/amphibians/frog.htm

Australian Museum
http://australianmuseum.net.au/image/Green-and-Golden-Bell-Frog-Life-cycle

Life Cycle of a Frog
www.tooter4kids.com/Frogs/life_cycle_of_frogs.htm

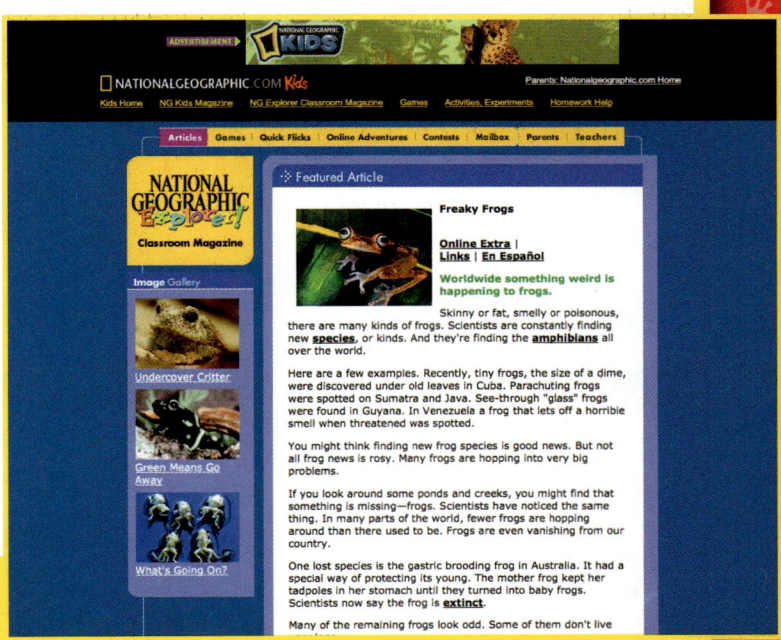

National Geographic Kids
http://magma.nationalgeographic.com/ngexplorer/0403/articles/mainarticle.html

Glossary

algae: a small, rootless plant that lives in the water

attract: to cause one to become interested in something

breed: have babies

burrow: to dig a hole in the ground to use as shelter

cold-blooded: to have a body temperature that changes to match the temperature of the places where one lives

froglets: tiny, young frogs

gills: organs that help animals breathe under water

metamorphosis: the process of changing from one stage of life to the next

organs: body parts, such as the heart or liver, that perform a specific job

oxygen: a gas that living beings need to breathe

predators: animals that hunt other animals for food

tadpoles: baby frogs that live in water, have a tail, and breathe through gills

vocal sacs: loose folds of skin on the sides of the mouth

Index

amphibians 4

eggs 7, 8, 10, 20, 22

froglet 7, 14, 22

hatching 8, 10

mating 7, 16, 20

tadpoles 8, 10, 13, 14, 22